Dear Parent: Your child's love of reading starts here!

Every child learns to read at his or her own speed. You can help your young reader by choosing books that fit his or her ability and interests. Guide your child's spiritual development by reading stories with biblical values. There are I Can Read! books for every stage of reading:

SHARED READING
Basic language, word repetition, and whimsical illustrations, ideal for sharing with your emergent reader.

BEGINNING READING
Short sentences, familiar words, and simple concepts for children eager to read on their own.

READING WITH HELP
Engaging stories, longer sentences, and language play for developing readers.

I Can Read! books have introduced children to the joy of reading since 1957. Featuring award-winning authors and illustrators and a fabulous cast of beloved characters, I Can Read! books set the standard for beginning readers.

Visit www.icanread.com for information on enriching your child's reading experience.
Visit www.zonderkidz.com for more Zonderkidz I Can Read! titles.

Queridos padres: ¡Aquí comienza el amor de sus hijos por la lectura!

Cada niño aprende a leer a su propio ritmo. Usted puede ayudar a su pequeño lector seleccionando libros que estén de acuerdo a sus habilidades e intereses. También puede guiar el desarrollo espiritual de su hijo leyéndole historias con valores bíblicos, como la serie ¡Yo sé leer! publicada por Zonderkidz. Desde los libros que usted lee con sus niños hasta aquellos que ellos o ellas leen solos, hay libros ¡Yo sé leer! para cada etapa del desarrollo de la lectura:

LECTURA COMPARTIDA
Utiliza un lenguaje básico, la repetición de palabras y curiosas ilustraciones ideales para compartir con su lector emergente.

LECTURA PARA PRINCIPIANTES
Este nivel presenta oraciones cortas, palabras conocidas y conceptos sencillos para niños entusiasmados por leer por sí mismos.

LECTURA CONSTRUCTIVA
Describe historias de gran interés para los niños, se utilizan oraciones más largas y juegos de lenguaje para el desarrollo de los lectores.

Desde 1957 los libros ¡Yo sé leer! han estado introduciendo a los niños al gozo de la lectura. Presentan autores e ilustradores que han sido galardonados como también un reparto de personajes muy queridos. Los libros ¡Yo sé leer! establecen la norma para los lectores principiantes.

Visite www.icanread.com para obtener información sobre el enriquecimiento de la experiencia de la lectura de su hijo.
Visite www.zonderkidz.com para actualizarse acerca de los títulos de las publicaciones más recientes de la serie ¡Yo sé leer! de Zonderkidz.

(Noah) sent the dove out from the ark again. In the
evening the dove returned to him. There in its beak
was a freshly picked olive leaf! So Noah knew that the
water on the earth had gone down.
–*Genesis 8:10–11*

(Noé) volvió a soltar la paloma fuera del arca. Caía la
noche cuando la paloma regresó, trayendo en su pico
una ramita de olivo recién cortada. Así Noé se dio
cuenta de que las aguas habían bajado hasta dejar la
tierra al descubierto.
—*Génesis 8:10-11*

Zonderkidz

Noah and the Ark/Noé y el arca
Copyright © 2009 by Mission City Press. All Rights Reserved. All Beginner's Bible copyrights and trademarks (including art, text, characters, etc.) are owned by Mission City Press and licensed by Zondervan of Grand Rapids, Michigan.

Requests for information should be addressed to:

Zonderkidz, *Grand Rapids, Michigan 49530*

Library of Congress Cataloging-in-Publication Data

Noah and the ark. Spanish & English
  Noah and the ark / illustrated by Kelly Pulley = Noé yel arca / ilustrado por Kelly Pulley.
    p. cm. -- (My first I can read! = Mi primer libro! ¡Yo sé leer!)
  ISBN-13: 978-0-310-71886-4 (softcover)
  1. Noah (Biblical figure)--Juvenile literature. 2. Noah's ark--Juvenile literature. 3. Deluge-Juvenile literature. I. Pulley, Kelly, II. title. III.
Title: Noé y el arca.
  BS580.N6N6218 2009
  222'.1109505--dc22

                                                                                                        2008051670

All Scripture quotations, unless otherwise indicated, are taken from the *Holy Bible: New International Reader's Version*®. NIrV®. Copyright ©
1995, 1996, 1998 by International Bible Society. Used by permission of Zondervan. All Rights Reserved.

Any Internet addresses (websites, blogs, etc.) and telephone numbers printed in this book are offered as a resource. They are not
intended in any way to be or imply an endorsement by Zondervan, nor does Zondervan vouch for the content of these sites and
numbers for the life of this book.

All rights reserved. No part of this publication may be reproduced, stored in a retrieval system, or transmitted in any form or by any
means—electronic, mechanical, photocopy, recording, or any other—except for brief quotations in printed reviews, without the prior
permission of the publisher.

Zonderkidz is a trademark of Zondervan.

Art Direction: Jody Langley
Cover Design: Laura Maitner-Mason

Printed in China

09 10 11 12 • 5 4 3 2 1

ZONDER**kidz**™ | **vida**®

I Can Read!™ | ¡Yo sé leer!™ | SHARED My First READING

Noah and the Ark
Noé y el arca

Genesis 6–9
Génesis 6–9

pictures by Kelly Pulley
ilustrado por Kelly Pulley

A long time ago, people were very mean to each other.
They forgot about God.

Hace mucho tiempo la gente era mala unos con otros.
Se olvidaron de Dios.

They did not love God.
This made God very sad.

No amaban a Dios.
Esto hizo que Dios se pusiera muy triste.

But Noah was a good man.
Noah and his family loved God.

Pero Noé era un hombre bueno.
Noé y su familia amaban a Dios.

God had a big plan. He told Noah,
"I am going to start over."

Dios tenía un gran plan. Le dijo a Noé:
«Voy a comenzar de nuevo».

God told Noah to build a boat.

Dios le dijo a Noé que fabricara un barco.

The boat was called an ark.

El barco se llamaba un arca.

And Noah did what God said.

Y Noé hizo lo que Dios le dijo.

God said, "I will save you.
I will save your family and two of
each animal."

Dios dijo: «Te salvaré.
Salvaré a tu familia y a dos animales
de cada especie».

Noah built the boat.
God sent the animals.

Noé fabricó el barco.
Dios mandó los animales.

"Hi, cats and dogs!
Hi, bears and birds!"

«¡Hola, gatos y perros!
¡Hola, osos y pájaros!».

There was food.
There was family.

Allí había comida.
Allí estaba la familia.

There were God's animals.

Allí estaban los animales de Dios.

One day, God closed the door.
Then God sent a big storm!

Un día, Dios cerró la puerta.
¡Entonces Dios envió una gran tormenta!

Rain began to fall.
It rained and rained.
The ark rocked and rocked.

Comenzó a caer la lluvia.
Llovió y llovió.
El arca se mecía y se mecía.

The ark bumped up and down,
up and down.

El arca brincaba para arriba y para
abajo, arriba y abajo.

Noah prayed.
Noah's family prayed.
The animals watched.

Noé oraba.
La familia de Noé oraba.
Los animales observaban.

God took care of Noah.
God took care of his family.

Dios cuidó a Noé.
Dios cuidó a la familia de Noé.

God kept all of them safe.

Dios los salvó a todos.

The rain fell for days,
and days, and days.

Llovió durante días
y días y días.

24

The earth was covered with water!

¡La tierra se cubrió de agua!

"Shhhhh," Noah said.
Something was different.

«Shhhhh», dijo Noé.
Algo era diferente.

It was quiet!
The rain had stopped!
The ark was still!

¡Había silencio!
¡Dejó de llover!
¡El arca se detuvo!

Noah said,
"Dove, please find land."
But Dove did not find land.

Noé dijo:
«Paloma, por favor busca la tierra».
Pero la paloma no encontró la tierra.

Noah said, "Dove, try again."
Dove did find land!

Noé dijo: «Paloma, vuelve a intentarlo».
¡La paloma encontró la tierra!

29

One day, the ark bumped into land.
Slowly, the water started drying up.

Un día, el arca chocó contra la tierra.
Poco a poco el agua se fue secando.

God said, "Time to go!"
He helped Noah open the ark.
The animals went to play.

Dios dijo: «¡Ya es hora de salir!».
Y ayudó a Noé a abrir el arca.
Los animales salieron a jugar.

God said, "See the rainbow?
It means I will not cover the earth
with water again. I promise!"

Dios dijo: «¿Ves el arcoiris?
El arcoiris es una promesa.
No volveré a inundar la tierra».

Floppy Mop

by Bobby Lynn Maslen
pictures by John R. Maslen

Scholastic Inc.

New York Toronto London Auckland Sydney

W9-AZT-500

Also available:
Bob Books®
for Beginning Readers

More Bob Books
for Young Readers

Even More Bob Books
for Young Readers

For more Bob Books ask for them at your local bookstore or call: 1-800-733-5572.

No part of this publication may be reproduced in whole or in part, or stored in a retrieval system, or transmitted in any form or by any means, electronic, mechanical, photocopying, recording, or otherwise, without written permission of the publisher. For information regarding permission, write to Scholastic Inc., 555 Broadway, New York, NY 10012.

ISBN 0-590-93810-X

Copyright © 1996 by Bobby Lynn Maslen.
All rights reserved. Published by Scholastic Inc.
BOB BOOKS is a registered trademark of Bob Books Publications.

12 11 10 9 8 7 6 5 4 3 2   6 7 8 9/9 0 1/0

Printed in the U.S.A.

First Scholastic printing, August 1996

Mop was a big dog.

Mop was a floppy dog.

Mop was Tom's pal.

"Come, Mop," said Tom.

Tom sat on Mop.

Jack was a cat.

Zack was a rat.

Zack ran. Jack ran after Zack.

Mop ran after Jack and Zack.

"Stop, Mop," begged Tom.
Mop stopped.

Mop and Tom sat.

Tom and Mop had a nap.

The End

List of 23 words in *Floppy Mop*

Short Vowels

a	o	i	e	irregular
cat	on	big	begged	a
rat	Mop			was
sat	Tom			said
nap	dog			come
ran	stop			
had	floppy			
and				
pal				
Jack				
Zack				
after				

58 total words in *Floppy Mop*